D1456899

BEAUTY ENTREPRENEURS

An insiders' guide on how to start a beauty
business, survive it and succeed in it

MICHELLE F. WILLIAMS

MICHELLE WILLIAMS GROUP LLC

ISBN: 978-1-4834-0085-3 (sc)
ISBN: 978-1-4834-0084-6 (e)

Because of the dynamic nature of the Internet, any web addresses or links contained in this book may have changed since publication and may no longer be valid. The views expressed in this work are solely those of the author and do not necessarily reflect the views of the publisher, and the publisher hereby disclaims any responsibility for them.

Lulu Publishing Services rev. date: 07/22/2013

*I want to dedicate this book to all the
inspiring entrepreneurs out there, some I
have met and many I have yet to meet*

A "how to" book that is a guide through the ups and downs of creating a beauty product business, giving tips on the best practices for success and what not to do

Contents

Chapter One

Notes From Me to You

If you have picked up this book to read, then I feel I already know you. I have been working with entrepreneurs from the beauty business for over 20 years. There are certain similar characteristics of people who decide to make a beauty product for commercial purposes. Like most of my clients, you may have no background in the beauty business or possibly any business.

You are passionate, even if it is just about your product. You are creative or have an inventive mind. Problem solving is also a strong trait and you often think of products for the beauty industry that are just not out there yet. I am often amazed at the "research skills" my clients use in order to get as far as they do in getting their business started. Often the first steps come just by using the internet and a "can do" attitude to get the job done. The unfortunate part is that you can't trust everything you read on the internet. And there are too many people giving advice that don't know what it is like to actually produce a beauty product and get it ready to show to retail buyers.

My experience covers 30 years in the various aspects of the retail business as a buyer and manager for a major department store chain whose corporate name was Federated Department Stores. I ultimately became a vice president of cosmetics for that corporation. Today it is known as Macy's and Bloomingdale's. Part of my experience was spent at Bloomingdale's stores as a buyer of fragrances. That was an exciting time. I learned a great deal during those years with great leaders in the retail business. I appreciated all the training I received on the corporate world of retail. However, being an entrepreneur was always in my blood. I had a reputation of being a bit of a rebel. I was always trying to push the envelope. That passion ultimately led me to become a consultant and create my own agency, The Michelle Williams Group, dedicated to working with entrepreneurs.

This guide is written essentially with my knowledge of the United States market in beauty. Although I have had various experiences with the beauty business in countries outside of the United States, in this book I am giving my perspective on the United States beauty business.

There is something about working with entrepreneurs that really makes me feel alive. Even with all the confusion out there, I find most of the people who come to me seeking my advice are able to figure out about fifty to seventy five percent of what is needed to get their business going. Their sheer determination drives them to make it happen up to a point. But then there is that point where they get stuck trying to figure out how to get it sold, or find an investor, or where to get their prototype made. I have found that the areas that get them stuck are varied. But it's uncanny how many of the "mistakes" people make when starting out are also very common amongst everyone. (More about that later in top 10 things not do to). By the time clients have found me for advice, they are often already disheartened by those mistakes or being stuck and are in serious need of direction. Avoiding the common errors is the key to preserving your energy for the good stuff.

The feeling that comes with succeeding in this business is as sweet as it gets . . . and fun. Don't get me wrong, it's hard work and figuring out what the customer wants at all times is a real challenge. So for those of you up for a challenge, you are in for the ride of your life. You may have already gone through some of these emotions already but if not, don't be surprised if you find that you have moments of "what was I thinking" to "I wonder if I will ever get this done". Of course there are those one in a million out of the gate successes that occur. I recommend to most of my clients that they need the virtue of patience while pieces of the puzzle come together. And they will come together. Keep your eye on the prize and keep checking in with yourself about "why" you are doing this. Don't listen to critics who warn you about failure. It's ok to have some days of doubt, but you have to shake it off and keep taking steps to get your product made and distributed out there. Surround yourself with the supportive friends, family and even suppliers, who can cheer you on when you have a bad day.

I think the creative process is exciting but filled with curves in the road that make you question your own ability. Oddly enough, every time I have felt that way in my own consulting business or worked with a client who thought it was over, I found that the desire to succeed would ultimately overcome those thoughts. And before you knew it, a new way of looking at the problem or inventive solutions would appear out of nowhere. So knowing that there may be those times you will experience, I recommend that you keep your thinking cap on and realize that answers will eventually come when you feel stuck or concerned. It's best not to let challenges get you or the ones around you down. See it as an obstacle that needs to be overcome and get back on track. Letting it get to you is truly a waste of your creative juices. Ok, enough of the pep talk about the challenges. Now let's get to the basics of getting started.

Chapter Two

"I Have This Idea"

Music to my ears: "I have this idea". I love to hear from people who want to share how they came up with their business idea. The answers are amazing to me. I can see why television sees this process as exciting enough to make weekly shows from it in one form or another.

Although many of the exciting beauty product ideas I have seen come from "problem solving", there are also the exciting design ideas that make an existing product seem new and fresh using new ingredients or a more beautiful packaging presentation. Some of the best business ideas come from taking a great product and simply making it better, more exciting. That may seem easier but it takes pure creativity to reinvent something.

First thing you need to do is write down a description of what your product or concept is. Describe it in as much detail as you can. What makes it different, why do you feel it is needed, does it fix a problem, why do you feel passionate about wanting to create it. The last question of "why" you want to do this is sometimes easier to explain after you have written all the details you can think of that make it exciting to you. When you write down the details, the idea becomes more real to you and that is important.

There is one idea that must be considered when you've decided to create a beauty product. Assuming that you've done some research that the product is unique and not necessarily out in the market the way you see it, you have to ask yourself why it does not exist. The answer actually may be because the consumer doesn't want it or need it. There is not always an easy answer to this question. Ask as many people you possibly can what they think about your product idea. Be sure to also review where you think it should be sold and why.

Name the baby. You are creating something so deciding on a name for the business or the product is very important. It's always helpful to have your product name give some clue about what the product does. I struggled myself to name my consulting business other names like "Ahead of the Curve" because it described the feeling I had about entrepreneurs. But ultimately I realized that people wanted to come to me for my experience and my name did have recognition in the beauty business. I realized that all those years on the retail side meant something to people that wanted to deal with someone that was credible. So my name won out and I simply called it the Michelle Williams Group. But I would advise if your product is "cool" or very unique . . . then don't be afraid to call it something unusual. I am sure we never thought we would be dealing in a global way with something called "GOOGLE". It even became a verb! Very unusual names also help when you start to think about search engines for web sites. The more unusual, the more likely you will come up on top in a search since you will not be like other names. You will be the one to make sure the name is memorable or the way you market it is memorable. But also remember that a name becomes the thing you need to have designed graphically (even if it is your own name) and it will need to be easy to say it or remember it. It might have a sound element to it as well. When you do name your business or product it should "feel" right to you. If not, then keep searching for one that does. Talk to friends about it, sometimes your inspiration can come from outside influences.

Now that you have your name, perform a trademark search on it. I think it's important to trademark the name of your product or business if it is unique. You can do this yourself just to get an idea of how many other people may already have that name or something close to it. Go to www. uspto.gov and choose "Trademarks" tab. Then choose "basic word mark search", it will be pre set to singular and plural and dead and live. For the first search leave it as is just to see what comes up. You can then narrow down to "Live" only etc. This gives you some idea who may already have the trademark or something close to it. Or, no one has it! And you can feel comfortable to register it on line at this site or contact a trademark lawyer. It's approximately a fee of $360 for one trademark in one "class of business". A common class category for beauty is "03". But there are many classifications depending on your business or service. There are people you can actually speak to at the U.S. Trademark offices. They can be helpful. They are running a business too. A trademark lawyer will charge you anywhere from $500 to $1000 depending. It varies from lawyer to lawyer. If you are not comfortable doing it yourself online, (I have done it many times) then seek out a trademark lawyer or go to the new legal websites where you can do it online and get some basic advice from lawyers that are associated with those sites. I am not a legal expert but I like to coach people to do some basic research themselves. It can help to do the basic searches on the USPTO site. Bottom line, there are ways to save money on the legal side of forming your business, from incorporating your company to trademarks and doing some of the basic legalities yourself is possible today. This is where information on the internet can be helpful. I want to point out that having a trademark doesn't mean that it may not be challenged by someone else who wants it and can possibly outspend you in lawyers. That is the tough aspect. You will have to be prepared to lawyer up in order to defend your right to your trademark name. I do think however, that having the name trademarked and getting to market first are ways to keep others that are smaller than the big guys from taking your name on their product illegally. It will make them think twice.

Business plans. I don't think business plans are meaningful unless you are looking for investors for your business. I know that goes against many "how to start" a business books and articles. Business plans do help you organize your expenses that you may incur to get your business up and running, but beyond that I have never seen a business plan be the reason an entrepreneur's business was successful, in the beauty business at least. You should be knowledgeable about what costs you are going to incur in order for you to get your business up and running. You should have a logo designed, get a sample (called a prototype) of your product and/or a properly designed website to explain your business. I will have more advice on the costs and where to find sources to make these, in the following chapters.

A note about Investors: I am often asked the question about the possibility of getting financial support from investors. The answer to that is fairly simple. Traditional investors or even your smart neighbor don't want to invest in businesses that are not up and running yet. Of course that might change if you have a very unusual idea or product, maybe a patented design etc. But in general it's very unusual to get an investor interested unless you can show them at least a year or so of financial performance of your business. There are various levels of investors. The ones that take on a business early are the real risk takers and for that level of risk they expect a large percentage ownership of your business for what amounts to be a modest investment in money. So be prepared for those kinds of conversations if you start to look for money in the early stage of your business. Whatever you do, don't mortgage the house! Some people get very caught up in the process of entering the beauty business and that can lead to problems. If you want to spend some of your savings in getting your business going then do it with careful consideration of what you can afford to spend. In my top 10 mistakes section of this book you will see my advice to not go and make inventory, especially too much inventory, before you know that you have potential buyers lined up. It's one of the biggest financial mistakes people make in the beginning of this process. I'm not a fan of involving a lot of friends and family but if they are willing to support you and you keep their financial commitment at reasonable levels, then they may be your greatest source of financial support. Be sure they understand the risk. Make sure you draw proper papers if you involve them in investing with your business.

Be sure of your timing also. Don't take funds you don't need or take it too early. If you find yourself doing that, then all you will be getting is frequent calls about what is happening and what progress have you made. There is a tendency to make your pitch to get funded into the next greatest business idea that ever came along. I often would listen to potential clients tell me that they are sure their product or business is going to be as phenomenal as . . . . (you fill in the blank). But you get my point I am sure. Just because you make a product that may be something like what Oprah called her favorite thing . . . does not mean that you are a candidate for the Oprah show. Just using this as an example of how great ideas can be pulled into the stratosphere rather than grounded in good common sense. Keep your vision high and of course dream big dreams but when it comes to investors, it's best to make your pitch be all about possibilities but with the knowledge it may take a bit of time to get where you are going with it.

Chapter Three

Top-Ten Mistakes

I am including my thoughts on the top-ten mistakes I have found in dealing with people starting out in the beauty business. I wrote and published these online a number of years ago. Many people have read them and given me feedback that they have found them very helpful. I feel some of these mistakes can be avoided and will save you money and time. So here is my article in its entirety.

As part of my advice to clients I always give them a list of the most common mistakes people make when they are entering into the beauty business. In fact, I have found many of these mistakes often apply to any category of start-up businesses. Over the years that I have been observing people who have become successful in the beauty business, there were so many different ways they went about achieving success, but when it came to the mistakes along the way, they seem to all share a number of the same ones. There is nothing wrong with making mistakes; in fact, you should be prepared to fail at some things as you go along. However, I feel strongly that you need to be prepared when entering the beauty business, and if you can avoid some costly pitfalls, you are at least ahead of the game. So to all the entrepreneurs out there, avoid these mistakes and you will be on your way!

(These are in no particular order of importance or sequence.)

1. **Hiring/paying for talent that is too expensive or too high level for things like graphics, advertising, designing of boxes, bottles, components, etc.**

Really do the research to find the experience you need without getting caught up in the "credentials" of these kinds of people. If the price seems crazy then keep looking, asking for recommendations for people they may know that could be more affordable since you are just starting out. It would also be best for you to look for people who have worked in the beauty industry.

2. **Pricing the "suggested price" of your product or service too high or too low.**

Be very smart (do your research)! It's about knowing who you think you want to have as your target audience to sell to, who is the end-user, who is your competition if any. You have to study what is out there and if your product is in the right price range considering all the variables that may make it different.

3. Producing too much inventory of your product before you have a potential buyer lined up.

I can't tell you how many people do this one step that puts them in a financial mess that is very difficult to work their way out of. Be sure to do everything you can to have potential buyers be able to see your product before you manufacture it in any significant quantity. Research how long it will take you to make your product so you can be ready to tell a buyer when you can ship to them. Many graphic people can help you with what is called a prototype product (a sample done well) that you can use to show buyers how you envision the product. Some retailers and buyers insist on seeing production quality, but you may just have to skip those particular people until you are really up and running in your business.

4. Producing too much inventory because the supplier you chose insisted on "minimums" that they will take as an order.

Do everything you can to search out suppliers that are willing to do "small runs." They may charge a bit more for each piece, but it is worth it if you are not taking on a large invoice for product that will take you too long to sell during your first phase of business. When you approach suppliers to make your products ask them up front if they are interested in working with smaller-quantity runs. Many suppliers who make product for the beauty industry, be it packaging, components, etc., deal with quantities of ten thousand or more. If you're just starting out you want to look for those who will work with you on quantities of less than five thousand, or even lower than one thousand. Be sure not to engage suppliers you may have found on the internet who are well known because those suppliers are going to look for large quantities only. There is one state in the United States that happens to be the place where a lot of manufacturers and warehouses are located—and that is New Jersey. But of course there are many others, and they tend to be located on the coasts of the United States.

5. **Designing your product, brochure, business card to be "too personal" instead of representing what the product or service is about.**

It's OK to have your package or brochure have your approach as part of it, but you are not designing your personal space at home, so be careful not to let your product be "over-designed." This can include simple things like having your package font in script when the customer can't easily read it, but you chose that font because you thought it looked "pretty." Or have text running up the side of the package. I think you get my drift; listen to your graphic artist if you have one or ask a lot of people if they feel the package or message is clear in what you want them to understand. Unless consumer design is part of your background, then you need to research what is out there to help your product or service stand out without being confusing to the customer.

6. Not having the operations worked out and not getting help to stay organized.

This aspect of any start-up is important. You should choose a small shipping facility if you are going to have a substantial business or be really prepared to handle it at home if you are up to it. There are a lot of details and learning curves here, but there are also many websites and books out there to help you get organized. If you stumble on the shipping or efficiency of your business, your clients will know and it will keep you from being recommended so be diligent about what you promise to do.

7. Not knowing why your product or service is special or different.

There are so many businesses competing for the same customer, you have to be sure that your product makes a difference that counts. Use friends, neighbors, and strangers if need be to form your own small focus group. If they are being honest and tell you they love the idea or would buy the product or service, you are getting responses to how the product is received. If they don't like it you have to accept that as well and figure out why they don't like it.

8. **Not doing your research on what the needs are of the potential business or customer to whom you are trying to sell.**

While I was a buyer of beauty in the department-store business, I often saw new suppliers who wanted to sell to my company, but when we sat down to review their products, they would ask me certain questions that made me realize they did not know much about my company and how we worked. Some questions are expected by the buyers, but if those questions reveal how little you know about the company you are selling to . . . it will not go well.

9. **Having unrealistic expectations, especially financially.**

It's easy to get overly excited about your new business, but I have witnessed very experienced people get caught up in expecting large financial results that will be difficult to meet and can be a big disappointment to yourself and others that may have invested money into your company. It's good to have a goal to "reach" for, but don't overdo it. Be willing to take one step at a time; it is a process.

10. **Getting thrown off course from the occasional disappointments and not staying focused.**

You must always rise above the occasional disappointments, fix the problems as they show up, and stay focused.

If you are really committed to seeing your business become successful then prepare yourself ahead of time to expect some disappointments. I have seen so many great ideas or businesses not get to their point of great returns because the owners were not thick-skinned enough to handle it when things did not go their way. They also become unfocused, losing sight of what they knew they could achieve. Don't lose focus.

Chapter Four

SUPPLIERS . . . The good, The bad, and the ugly

I am going to tell you what I know about dealing with suppliers. I feel that I will never know enough about this area, but I will share with you what I have learned since I started consulting with entrepreneurs who are creating product. I know that whomever you choose as your suppliers: the printers or the manufacturers of the product itself can absolutely make or break your business. It's obvious that you want to choose a supplier that produces quality work. The problem I see often with clients that I work with in the beginning is that they may have already started the process with suppliers that were not very good. Or even worse, they paid a supplier a lot of money to manufacturer too much product based on a supplier's insistence that they produce large minimums as they are referred to in the business.

When people get caught up in dealing with the suppliers, they buy more product than they need so that their price per piece will be less. You don't want to get caught up in that cycle especially when you're just starting out. Paying a bit more per piece by producing less quantity gives you the flexibility to change things as you go forward without feeling like you're stuck with a heavy quantity of inventory.

Good suppliers come in all sorts of forms. They could be very good because they are very big and handle well-known brand names, but that doesn't necessarily mean that is the right supplier for you. There are many good suppliers that will produce moderate quantities of inventory for you and still produce a quality product. Yes, you will have to do a bit more research to find them, but it will be worthwhile in the end. Often, there are suppliers who use sales representatives to help them find business, and those sales representatives rely heavily on commissions for the business they bring in. I'm not saying that sales representatives are the bad guys (or gals), but I have often found their agenda is to just make the sale versus finding clients that will give them the long-term business from a good relationship. I have often found it helpful when I am able to meet the owner of the facility that I am considering making a product with. When I see the owner is accessible and involved in his or her business I feel they have more focus on making sure they make a good product. The suppliers you meet with might have clients that have been with them from the beginning of making the product and still are with them after building their business together. When a supplier can give you a few examples of clients they have helped to build, then you probably have found a good supplier to start with. At some point when businesses become really large, it is necessary to find facilities that have the ability to make larger quantities. That's perfectly normal. But the people that helped you in the beginning are crucial to your success.

The financial aspects of starting up with a supplier can be difficult in the beginning because most suppliers want to be assured that the costs of the raw materials they will have to buy in order to fill your order will be covered by a deposit up front. They have found themselves too often in a situation in which they have bought those materials for a client who ends up not paying them because their business never got off the ground. I often recommend negotiation in this area of deposits. I like to suggest 30 percent of the invoice to be paid up front, 30 percent upon delivery, and 40 percent thirty days after the delivery. This way, the supplier has most of their costs covered and some of their profits. Many suppliers prefer to have 50 percent up front and 50 percent upon delivery, but that's not giving you an opportunity and time to sell your product and have some cash-flow. Try to find suppliers who are willing to work with you. I had been somewhat successful in dealing with suppliers that like to make larger quantities such as ten thousand pieces or more and have asked them to ship and bill me only on partial quantities of ten thousand pieces until I have completed asking for the entire quantity made. Some suppliers will do this for you, but they don't volunteer it up front.

Be sure to be prepared to have some financial statements, be it business or personal, with you so you can show the supplier you are financially sound. Be prepared to also share with them your business ideas for starting your company and who your customers will be. Your suppliers are like your silent partners in a way. If they believe in you, they will help you to become successful by offering you additional creative ideas and resources of people they know that can also help you. Be sure to ask your suppliers to give you quotes on the cost of doing the smallest amount they are willing to do, be it one thousand pieces or lower and then what the prices will drop to in larger quantities. I will tell you in my own experience that I have seldom been able to negotiate these prices of quotes down once they are given. What you can do is obtain quotes from a few suppliers and see if you can put the best two quotes into a competitive bidding situation. At the end of the day you just want to make sure you're working with the supplier who has the best quality and who also stands behind their work. Be sure to ask the suppliers you work with how you will be assured that the product quality will be there when they go into production. What are their policies when something does go wrong? Get all of this in writing if you can. Also be sure that you're not working with a middleman. By this I mean a company that has set themselves up to subcontract the work to make boxes or components and final products. There are many of these kinds of companies in the United States, in particular. Avoid them. They are simply fronts for other manufacturers.

Whatever you do, be sure that you stay involved in the process of your product being made. The more that the supplier feels that you're on top of your business; the more comfortable they will be in working with you. Many clients of mine that found the supplier told them what they wanted, and then just assumed that everything would turn out fine. Whenever possible, ask for prototypes or initial sample pieces to be shown to you before they go into actual production. They may ask you to pay a bit more money to be able to have these samples ahead of time, but in many cases it will be worthwhile. If you are communicating a lot by email with them, be sure to save every email or correspondence. Be very specific in your communication and if you don't understand any of the language that they are using with you, such as trade terms, then ask them to explain it to you or do some research online so you know what they are talking about.

I have often thought about creating a rating guide for suppliers in this industry, much like we use the Zagat guide to find restaurants. It would make it so much easier for entrepreneurs in the beauty business to get started. But that will have to be another project of mine.

A few thoughts on your components (lipstick cases, compacts, tubes, jars, bottles, and caps) : You should be looking for "stock" components. Do not even consider having a custom-molded component made—too expensive. Today there are enough creative decorative opportunities for stock components to help your product look uniquely yours. Bottles can be a bit trickier but you can make customized caps that, although they are still comparatively expensive to mold (for example, about$25,000), if your brand is about a fragrance line, then it's worth having your bottle cap be your own. Tubes and jars can be customized by using really good labels to wrap around the tube or around a jar. Visit some suppliers and do your investigation. I am sure you will find some great alternatives to make your products look unique.

Chapter Five

Who Is Your Customer?

Once you are clear on what your product or business is, you have a name, and you have figured out how to legally protect it, you will need to figure out where you are going to sell it and at what price. For the beauty business, in most cases, you will need to develop your wholesale price and your "suggested retail price" (SRP) for your product. I will go into more details on this in the following chapters.

You should begin to plan where you think you will want to sell your product or service. At least have an idea if you are thinking of your product in the lower-priced "mass" business (for example, Target, Walmart, chain drugstores), large chain stores that are moderately priced in product offerings, or the department store business, or high-priced stores. You may also be thinking of your product being right for only ecommerce selling. Or you may be one of the great new break-outs of a new product on a TV shopping channel!

Once you have the customer in mind that you want to sell to then you can begin to plan out the way you will package it or design the container for it (very, very important). Visual impressions are extremely important in this business. Too much design and it looks cheap, too little and it may be something the customers miss altogether. You are also going to need some advice on what you have to put on the package and where, in regard to size of the product, where the product is shipped from, the legal name of the company that makes it, etc. Some of this can be found on the internet, but I like to take a lot of products from reputable brands and follow their lead. The bigger companies have many people working on these issues, so I tend to think if there was a regulation for the package, then the big guys are making sure they follow it. Your supplier making your products may also be able to help out here.

I often have people contact me for advice on the process of where to sell their product. I frequently find that they have not done any research on this. You have to start to look at prices, design, and packaging in the places you hope to sell to. Try to find "benchmarks" of brands or products you want to emulate. This will give you someplace to start. Really look at the design and packaging of a product and what the selling price is. I often find clients who want to price their product at the high end, but they have packaged the product very cheaply because they are trying to save some money or went to the wrong supplier to get the job done and they paid too much. Buyers in better stores will see through this right away. Everything in the beauty business is visual.

You also need to take into account the "amount" of product you are going to be selling versus the competition. So the volume of the lotion being five ounces or seven ounces will matter, or selling two lipsticks versus three in a package. All these details add up to whether your product is priced right for the right customer and whether it looks the part of the place you want to sell into. If you only hope to sell on a website or television shopping channel then you may have it a little easier on the packaging issues. I will explain more in detail later when I break out the details of dealing with different retailers, but for now, let me just say there is less scrutiny on packaging from these types of retailers.

I believe that most of my clients have always been somewhat surprised by who they find as their core customers. Surprised because they thought it was one kind of customer, only to find out it is another. So it will be interesting once you start to show your product and start selling it to find out what type of customer you have captured.

Chapter Six

Ready, Set, GO!

Well, by now you may have figured out your product, its pricing, its packaging, and your logo. You may or may not know who your customer is. You now have to get it sold and distributed to retail. When I refer to the word *retail* in this previous sentence, I mean stores, websites, catalogs . . . . anywhere that will be buying your product from you (at wholesale price) and then selling it at their retail price. The difference of which is their profit. Your profit is the difference of the wholesale price you sell at versus the price it cost you to make the product.

In some cases, you may sell at different wholesale prices. You may offer discount pricing for large-volume purchases. You may decide to make a specific product in your range of different ones that will have a special pricing at wholesale because you are making it exclusively for the retailer you are selling to. But there is something about the beauty business that is somewhat unusual in the pricing of products. In the beauty category, it is often the practice to sell your product based on a discount percent off of what you establish as your Suggested Retail Price, commonly called SRP. So let's say you have made a product that costs you $2.00 to make (the complete package and product). The retailers buying the beauty category want to know what you state as your SRP and then they tell you what they expect to make in profit as a rule by telling you the "margin" they need to make. Using an easy example, you will say your product has a SRP of $10.00, and they want to have a 50 percent margin . . . so they will be buying it at $5.00. In this case, you are making a gross profit of $3.00. There are the other costs of doing a business which end up affecting your bottom-line net profit, but that is another chapter to review later.

I can't tell you how this SRP approach was adopted into the industry of beauty products, but I know it is used in other categories as well. In the industry of beauty, it creates a way for retailers to be able to sell the products at a stable price that most retailers use. It then puts them onto an even playing field to keep the price at the SRP. By law it is every retailers' right to price the retail price at what they want to after they have purchased the goods. Some may go higher than your SRP if they are a small store and they are not worried about competition having the same product. Some may want to go lower, but it is generally not what most retailers want to do unless they are a discount store. Most retailers want to be at the SRP price.

How do you come up with the SRP for your product? You look at your product in the scheme of the market. What is the going price for a product like yours selling for? If there is nothing else like it then you may also take into consideration the retailer that you are targeting to sell to. If they are a high-end store, then they are generally looking for "better-priced" or higher-priced products. A "mass store" (a term used for lower-priced products in stores like pharmacy chains or discount chains of stores) will be looking for lower, value-priced type of products. You should also look at the price it cost you to make it. If your research tells you that you are going after a high-end-priced customer and retailer to sell it, then you need to price your product high. A "rule of thumb" in the business is to aim for costs of your product to be no more than 10 percent of your SRP. But in smaller start-up businesses, it is rare you can achieve that low a "cost of goods." It's more common to be at a 20 to 30 percent of SRP. If you see that you feel your product is clearly meant to sell at say $100.00, and your costs to make the product are adding up to $40.00, then you need to ask yourself if you can raise the retail price and still hold the interest of the consumer to buy it at that price or look at ways that you can reduce your costs. Of course, how you intend to use the profit you are making will be a factor. You may be able to ship products from your home (I rarely recommend that) or hire family to help get the labor done you need, etc. These costs in relation to putting your product into the market may be something a good accountant can help you with. But the price you believe is right for your product, and the market to make it successful are key factors to what the costs of your products need to be.

Once you have worked on some of these details, get an order form printed or create it as an electronic file that you can send via emails. The order form should have your logo at the top of the page; your address and contact info is also necessary. Make a clear, easy-to-read graph of information for each of your products, line by line, what the style number is (I like five-digit style numbers) and what the UPC (Universal Product Code) is for each. You can Google how to get UPC codes to understand this better. Then put the SRP. If you are selling mainly to people who are asking for 50 percent margins (common in boutique-type retailer) then you can make a column just for those retailers that includes the wholesale cost of each product. If you have policies you want to make as part of your shipping and returns, etc., then I would include them at the bottom of the order form. Many retailers, especially websites and catalog companies, ask you to sign their agreement form, which will state their policies in doing business with you. Many points are negotiable so *ask* them to change anything that you feel you can't agree to before signing. They will tell you the areas that are non-negotiable.

Larger stores like department stores and chains may not ask for agreements to be signed but rather have a letter of agreement that states what you have both agreed upon other than the costs of the products (which will be on a purchase order that they will issue to you). They often have what they call "routing guidelines" that they give to you, which simply state the policy of how they want you to ship the product and to where. For example, they may have some restrictions on how small a box can be based on their distribution centers' (warehouses) receiving systems. It always sounds more complicated than it really is, but a good warehouse can explain this to you or will just take care of it.

It's good to have a general sense of the terminology of some stores and the rules for how they take you on as a new vendor It's OK to ask questions, but anything you can learn about prior to meeting with a buyer is helpful. If you act too green in what your questions are, it can create a concern with the buyer that you are not capable of handling the business. Try to avoid that.

Chapter Seven

Getting to the Buyer

Most people who approach me for help are confused or intimidated by how to reach out to the buyers in retail establishments. It is not as difficult as you think. I was a buyer for many years for a major department store chain in New York and I often had people call or email me to get an appointment to show their products to me. But if the product or brand was intriguing to me, I made time to see them.

I often meet clients who are extremely creative and who have a lot of passion about their product or company. But then they tell me they don't consider themselves salespeople. I understand that it's not always comfortable for people to turn themselves into a sales machine. If this is a challenge for you, you're going to have to prepare for this before you even make the inventory. You can get some training from someone who can help you with your presentation style and then practice, practice, practice, or you can find someone to be the salesperson for the company. I believe most entrepreneurs are not prepared financially to hire salespeople for their business unless they find someone just as entrepreneurial as they are. I will give you some advice on the subject from the perspective of the buyer meeting with either someone who was not sure of themselves or someone who isn't close to the creation of the product. Both kinds of people always feel awkward in the meeting. I would prefer to meet with the creator of the product, but in certain circumstances that person is truly not cut out for the business side of presenting their own products. So be very sure if you are not going to get better at it then be sure of the person who is going to do it for you. If on the other hand, you are comfortable with selling, then just be sure that you be yourself and know your product backwards and forwards. Don't be nervous; it's a waste of energy. And don't be overly enthusiastic—that makes the buyer think you are trying too hard.

I am going to give you a brief description of how to get thru to buyers and what steps to take ahead of time to help raise their interest to make an appointment with you or simply contact you.

1. Simplest and most common is to find out their name and email and send them a brief description of your

product or brand and its pricing. If you have press from magazines then send that along with the email. Remember: buyers are very busy people, but that does not mean that they are not looking for the next best thing or something that will make a difference in the assortment of product they carry presently. Be sure to find the buyer of your product category: be it fragrance, skincare or cosmetics, or now personal care in some stores. In many small single-store operations, there is only one buyer and often an assistant, or a clerical person. In that case you just need to get to him or her. I like to use social networks like Linked In ™ or Facebook ™ to search for people who are buyers for the area in the stores that I want to reach. You may have to start there to reach out or simply call the main number of the company that you are trying to reach. Their policy may be to simply allow for emails to be given out, not phone numbers. But the idea that they have no policy to reach buyers is silly. These stores have people in those jobs for a reason.

2. Get the address to send a sample to and include a concise letter on letterhead that introduces you and your product and all the information that is helpful. But *do not* overdo it. These buyers are busy and can only look at so much material. Also don't send three pieces or more of each product. That is something that drives buyers a little crazy. If they love the product they will contact you and ask you to bring more.

3. Once you have sent the sample (if you have enough to send) then follow up with another email asking if they have had a chance to look at the product and that you want to have the opportunity to meet them and present your line in more detail. If you don't have the luxury of a lot of samples to send then I would suggest you send an email with a photo of the product or brand and its pricing and where else you have sold it to, if anyone. They may or may not respond to that, but if the photos of the product look great or the link to your website is exciting and informative, they can often make a decision off that. Don't stalk buyers with repeated calls or emails. Instead, space them out and leave messages that are friendly and brief. If there is silence after a number of attempts then most likely they are not interested and possibly can't find the time to say no to you. I think this is a major issue for some buyers in some stores. They should find ways to get back to people, but I am just giving you a heads-up.

4. Some buyers are product junkies, and some are more into the marketing aspect of a brand. So be prepared. Some may want to ask detailed questions about skincare products while others may just love the packaging and will ask more questions about PR that you intend to do. Don't make the mistake of pushing details about clinicals on your products or ingredient issues that are too detailed. You will lose their attention. If it takes you that long to sell

the product, imagine how they feel it will be for the staff in their stores to sell it. Have a brief, focused description about your product differentiation and why it would add to the assortment they already carry (do your research in their stores or online).

5. Know how you will be able to give information or training to their staff. Many retailers will accept videos now, or take concise training books if necessary. Explain "who" from your company can do the training if needed. If it is you, the founder and creator, then I suggest you have a fifteen- to twenty-minute DVD already done by the time you speak to a buyer. They may ask to see it.

6. Shipping is a big issue to larger chains but being able to ship complete and on time is important to every retailer. Be prepared to say where you ship from and if they can handle EDI (electronic data input) or a fancy way of saying electronically taking an order from a store to your warehouse. Many larger stores use this software today versus the old hard-copy paper order. A good warehouse will be able to provide this, but there are extra costs associated with setting up with each retailer that you sell to. As a general rule, most retailers expect to pay the shipping fee to get the products to them. That policy you would set is referred to as FOB the warehouse. It means "freight on board" (strange term, I know) and then from "where," So FOB warehouse as your shipping policy to a buyer is to say that they will pay

the shipping from your warehouse. Many places that are located on the West Coast have requests to have the manufacturer pay the shipping for them since so many shipping locations are coming from the East Coast, and it becomes a costly fee for them. But that can often be negotiated.

7. How to approach the buyer: Most people think it is very difficult to get through to a buyer for an appointment. But it is actually far easier than you would think. All buyers need to buy product that is interesting and new. I recommend you start with a press kit. For those of you who don't know what a press kit is, I will give a brief explanation. It starts with a basic folder that you can often find in stationery stores. Try to choose one that has a color close to a color in your product or your packaging. These folders generally have two sides: on the left place information about your product and any press releases that you may have designed. On the right insert any photos of your product or copies of press that you may have already received and include a purchase order form. You can create a simple order form using your logo at the top of the page with your address and a simple graph below that allows you to enter the style number, and the UPC number (you will need to have UPC numbers for each of your products). Some retail stores will not require you to have UPC numbers, but that is generally for the smaller stores. Therefore, I believe it is helpful to have these prepared just in case you come

across a retailer who does need them. You should have a column next to each product that shows the suggested retail price and the wholesale cost (if you have established the wholesale cost), otherwise leave blank to be filled then by the retailer once you have established what their margins are. If you are able to put a nice-looking label on the front of the press kit then add that on. It's important to keep everything branded with your logo and the look of your brand. And always be consistent in how you use the graphic look of your logo.

These are some basics in preparing to reach out to a buyer, but they do speak more to the larger group of retailers. If you are just starting out and you are not up to producing thousands of pieces of product yet, then I recommend you start small at first. Single-store owners, referred in the industry as independents or boutiques, are a good, safe way to start selling your products if their store assortment or customer type is good for your brand. The owner is often the buyer and manager and is hands-on in terms of what products work and what products don't. They know their customers, and they are often looking for new things to try out. They run on smaller budgets to buy product but will start with a number of pieces to see if they work for their store. They may ask you to guarantee taking product back if it doesn't work (often called a guarantee-sale arrangement). If it is just six to twelve pieces, it is often worthwhile to say yes to this as long as the returns are in good condition to take back. These boutiques often buy with credit cards, versus asking for "terms" of thirty days to pay from date of receiving the products. You should go with taking their credit card since many of the smaller businesses are not always stable enough to pay invoices on time with cash. If they are a great local apothecary or pharmacy in your area and you know them, then offering them thirty days to pay for the products after receipt is not a risk generally. I feel the combination of creating your own website and having a few independents to get your feet wet is the best way to go in just starting out. It gives you a chance to feel what the customers like and if the stores can sell your product . . . and if not, why. Then you can make adjustments to pricing or do some creative values on your own website and see what happens.

It's better to do that adjusting early with a smaller group than to find out you were wrong on the price after selling to a big chain. Buyers in larger stores or websites are not always as good at understanding what price is good or bad on any brand. They are not traditional buyers like there are in the fashion or accessories business. Most of the products that department stores buyers are dealing with are from larger companies and pricing is clearly determined well before it is presented to a buyer. They do understand how a range of prices puts your product in a certain category of other products they sell, and that can be helpful in determining your competition.

In general the beauty buyers in larger stores know very little about the pricing of products. They are often people who execute (buy) what is going on in trends in the beauty business or determining how to market to reach a bigger audience for their stores. So if you are looking for answers about what you are doing right in pricing products, I would recommend you get your research in other places. On this note, I would also take with a grain of salt any personal liking or dislikes that a buyer may have toward packaging. They can run in many different directions. A good buyer no matter who they are buying for will see the commercial reasons why something will work in packaging regardless of their personal tastes. So steer away from questions like "Do you think you should do the box in brown or black"? Those questions are better left to your graphic designer.

Or try showing your packaging to lots of people on a paper drawing of them in either suggested color and get a consensus.

Some things to keep in mind in reaching out to buyers:

- Don't call buyers on Monday mornings. They are usually reviewing sales from the week before.
- Reach out to buyers early in the morning or late in the afternoon. The majority of their day is crammed with meetings and preparing reports.
- Never stalk buyers with constant calls made too close to each other. Buyers hate that. However, calling or

dropping an email once a month to check in and ask if there is an opportunity to make an appointment or reconsider taking in your brand is OK.

- Buyers plan their new brands to take in each season (there are two in the retail world: spring and fall). They plan to review in March for new brands to bring in the fall (starting July), and for spring they plan in October for shipments starting in January. A plan of buying for two seasons a year is generally used by department stores or chain stores. Many individual stores will purchase products throughout the year. However, the holiday season from about mid-October through end of December is generally not a time that any stores want to stop to look at new product.

You can probably see by now that going to large department stores or mass chains is not your best approach when first starting out. I don't want to say it's impossible either, just in case you are actually able to sell to these types of companies. Just be prepared to present to larger retailers. The buyers can spot a newbie from a mile away.

Planners: I think it is important for me to mention something about planners. These are generally individuals who are found in larger retail stores. When technology entered into retail it became obvious that an additional person would be needed to interact with the financial plans that each buyer develops for their assigned business each season. The planners are the people who actually organize and issue the purchase orders. They also make sure that the business remains on plan and that inventory to reach the sales goals is controlled. You may or may not be introduced to the planner when meeting with the buyer. As you start in a relationship with the store and the buyer you may eventually know the planner. If your business evolves you will want to request quarterly or seasonal meetings with the buyer and planner to review how your business is being funded with the inventory. In industry terms you don't want your stock turnover too fast. The planners don't want your stock to turn too slow. This is an area that you learn to work with as you grow your business with the store that has planners involved. Your point person to discuss business with will always be the buyer first.

Once you have your press kit set up then you can prepare to send it to buyers you want to reach out to along with samples of your product. If your samples are not *production quality*, then don't send them. There are companies you can hire to make production quality samples for you. In the business we call these *comps*. Of course if you have made inventory for your brand already you will be sending samples from production of inventory. Be sure to send the samples via FedEx or UPS. You want your package to arrive so that someone needs to sign for it; this way you will know it arrived, and the buyer will notice a FedEx or UPS package more than a simple brown box. Be careful not to overpackage the sample and press kit. By this I mean don't put it in a pretty box inside with ribbon or personal notes unless it is on your company stationery. You don't want this presentation to look like a gift. You are trying to approach these buyers to do business with. Let the brand speak for itself along with its logo and packaging.

You want to send the samples and press kit to the buyer's proper name and title and of course the correct address of their office. As I mentioned before, most buyers' names and addresses can be found through a little bit of work on the internet or calling a corporate office to ask for the information. The corporate offices generally don't like to give you a phone number to a buyers' office but will often give you their emails. Once you have sent your packages to the buyers' attention, follow up with an email to them giving them information about the approximate date the sample should arrive. Thank them in the email in advance for their time in looking at your brand. Let them know you would like to follow up with an appointment or phone call if they find the product interesting.

This approach of sending samples and press kits to buyers would be true for small stores as well as large ones. But you can approach small stores with simply information and photos via email. It can be costly to send samples to every store you would like to approach. Of course, you can contact a buyers' office and go directly to a request to have an appointment to make your presentation of your brand. It has been my experience that most people want to sample a product before they make these appointments with you. At the very least they want to see the product and information before meeting with you. Buyers often don't have a lot of time to spare in their week, and they need to be sure to allocate time for new products only when they believe the product will fit into their mix and that they have an interest in trying it. Occasionally you will have buyers say yes to a meeting once they have seen some basic information via email.

PRESS

If you have been lucky enough to get some press on your product in a magazine, for example, be sure to include a copy of that information in your email. Many stores today rely heavily on the press that is in magazines or newspapers as a benchmark for their interest level to carry the product. So press or what we refer to as PR plays a major role in the beauty business.

Not everyone is going to feel comfortable with the expense of hiring a PR company or person. The expense of this kind of service can run anywhere from $1,000 a month to $10,000 a month. You can sometimes find people who will charge you based on each piece of press they get for you. Individuals who run their own press business can also be hired to help you create a press release about your brand or products that you've created. Various types of press agents or people that dabble in this work usually have some sort of website presence. Search the internet for the words "public relations" in your town.

Chapter Eight

—— ✿ ——

Selling Your Products on Shopping Channels

Many people think that it's impossible to sell on shopping channels or at the very least it's difficult to get to the buyers. It's actually not as difficult as you might think. There are three major shopping channels in the United States today. Their names are QVC, HSN, and ShopNBC (soon to be called ShopHQ). For the beauty category of business, QVC and HSN are much bigger than ShopNBC. But since ShopNBC is the smaller one, it tends to be hungrier for the business and more flexible. I have had clients who started on ShopNBC and moved over to HSN. But clearly there are brands that have grown at ShopNBC and remain there.

Reaching out to buyers at the shopping channels is relatively straightforward. Much like department stores there are different buyers for each category. Generally there is one for cosmetics or color products; one for fragrances; one for skincare and sometimes one for personal care. Generally, there are assistant buyers in each of these categories as well. One way or another, there is someone to reach to ask for time to be able to present your product. The buyers like to receive product ahead of time so that they can get to know your business before giving you an appointment to present to them. I will point out to you that my experience with presenting to these buyers is that everything is on a time schedule. They are usually buttoned up about how much time they will be able to give you to present. It's generally an hour but be prepared for it to be less. You should practice points of your business and how you will convince them that it's an important product for them to put on air.

I have a word of caution about "brokers." These are people that are often sought out to hire in order to get your product in front of television shopping buyers. I caution people before engaging their services or signing any contracts with them. They seem to be a necessary evil in some cases for shopping channel buyers who prefer not to deal with inexperienced people when it comes to the way shopping television works. Many of these "brokers" advertise on the internet or come by word of mouth. They generally want to take 10 percent of your value of the wholesale sales you do on any given show. That is reasonable if they are helping you fill out the paperwork and getting you some training on how to go on air and do a good job. But I have a problem when they ask for clients to sign these agreements for no reasonable ending period. They might also tend to feel their job is done once they get your product on air. They have no jurisdiction to get you "more" airtime, but they tend to give the impression initially that they can. Their loyalty is to the stations and the buyers, not to you. So when things seem to go wrong, you will hardly see them in your corner. They are often previous people who had a big brand on air and then it ran its course so they were no longer needed on air . . . so they become instant "brokers" because they knew how the system works. Like everything in life, there are exceptions, but be very cautious of using these people as the only way you think you can get on air. I consult for people who want to go on air and do introductions of the product to buyers and also take a percentage of sales, but I don't do it for more than one-year time periods, renewable upon request. I also believe the client is the one I am supporting when things seem to go wrong, not the TV station. I am very concerned if my client is not seeing the best results, and we sit down and figure out why. Below are a number of other important points about television shopping and how it works.

There are a number of reasons why selling to a shopping channel is different from selling to a department store or catalog or even a website. But the most important aspect that makes them different is that they are buying their airtime from a television station and need to produce a certain amount of business to make a profit off of that expense. So they use a measure of success that they call dollars per minute or DPM. I'm going to list some basic points here about dealing with a shopping channel. It's not complicated to deal with shopping channels, but many people get intimidated by the details. I can assure you that it is not all that complicated, but there are some things you need to know that make it different from a regular retailer.

- Shopping channels generally don't buy your merchandise; they take it on consignment. This means they give you a purchase order of how many pieces they want you to ship and when, but they do not pay you for that merchandise until you have had a show and sold.

- Multiple forms are required to fill out in order to submit your products for sale on air. There is the typical vendor-agreement form, which is what they use to set your company up in their financial system. The real detailed forms come with providing them a lot of information on your products. They ask for the positioning of your brand, what makes it different, what are the key points that you would want to be sure to say on TV, or any claims you have about your products. These forms are not complicated, but they can be tedious.

- Quality control or approval of these forms and your product are looked at by a specific department at each shopping channel. The people in this department look at your product in every detail and the claims that you make on your forms. Shopping channels are under stricter regulations by the Federal Trade Commission (FTC) because they are on television. If you have something like a skincare line or want to make a lot of big claims about what your product does, then just be prepared to back it up. Generally these quality-control areas ask for tests to be done by a minimum of thirty participants to show the improvement that took place because of using the products. This is generally used for skincare or personal-care products where you want to make claims.

- Before and after photos of people who are using the product is an important piece to have available when you present your products to the buyers. It's not always necessary, but it's often a big selling point on television.

- You have to have someone who can present your brand on air, which they call the guest. They will request some sort of short video that will show them that the guest is capable of being on air. If not, they will recommend that training be secured or a substitute guest be available. They prefer to work with the creator of the brand.

- Shopping-channel pricing is all about value. If you are selling your product at a suggested retail price of $35, be prepared to offer them a discount from that price for on-air selling. They also like to offer multiple products at a special price that is something they are offering exclusively on their station.

- If you're on one shopping channel station you cannot be on others in the United States. Since there are only three channels in this media of business they are very competitive and ask that you remain exclusively with them. You can move from one station to the other as long as you have not signed an agreement, which you should not do unless you are completely sure you want to stay with the station offering you the agreement.

There are many other details to selling to a shopping channel. But these bullet points give the overview of what it is like to deal with shopping channels. There are challenges to working with shopping channels, but I feel the overall benefit is worth getting past the difficulties. You have to understand that television shopping has a higher level of risk than some more traditional forms of retailing. When it goes well it can be very lucrative, but when it goes bad you can find yourself taking back a lot of inventory that you had hoped to sell.

One other small oddity about selling your product on shopping channels is the lack of their focus on your primary packaging. Because it is TV, anything that has some color to it of course shows up better on TV than something that's a bland gray or white. But what TV is selling is what's *inside* the packaging and of course, *you*, if you're going to be the guest speaking about your product. The package becomes far less important than it is when you're showing a buyer who handles a regular store where packaging is extremely important. So if you're thinking of selling on TV alone, as your only point of distribution, then you may want to consider a cheaper packaging then you would if you were selling to a department store. Just something to keep in mind as you go about creating your total image.

Chapter Nine

Branding a Beauty Product: Image Is Everything

Assuming that you've developed a product that you're proud to put your name on, the most important part of the beauty product is how it is branded. The word branding can encompass a lot of things including the logo, the name of the product, a tagline, the way it's packaged, price of it, and the overall look of it.

Unless you are considering selling your product to mass stores, such as inexpensive chain stores or drugstores, then you have to put a lot of focus on what your product looks like. It is obviously the first thing that the buyer sees when you go to make your presentation. In my experience in the years I was a buyer in retail and the years I've consulted entrepreneurs, I have often found that the brand's owner was almost too focused on the product itself instead of making sure that the message of quality in the product was connected to the outer packaging. Products in the fragrance category and the color cosmetics category are easier for a buyer to make a quick assessment about in terms of the product itself. Skincare and body-care products are more difficult because there are no instant reactions except for possibly the scent of the skincare or body-care and the texture of the ingredients. But regardless of which category, your image is essentially your calling card for the brand to get noticed.

We live in the world today of high-tech in televisions, videogames, movies, computers, cars, and much more. Whether we like it or not, we have been trained to look at things with a discerning eye. Unless you are a graphic artist, this area of branding to help create your image and sell your product calls for a professional graphic artist to be involved. You want to be sure you're working with a graphic artist who understands packaging especially for the beauty business if at all possible. Instead of making it up from nowhere in your mind or just doing things like choosing your favorite color, I would recommend going out to purchase or print images of products that you feel you resonate with in the way that they look in the beauty industry. This way you'll have some place to start from when you engage the services of a graphic artist that you feel understands what you're looking for. I have seen a lot of new product lines presented to me in my career of many years in this industry. This area of packaging is where I found most startups miss this key element of image. In general people tend to want to overdesign their packaging and put too much of their personal style into it. If there is a story behind the product they also like to add too many details onto the package. You have to remember that the space that you're designing on in most cosmetic products is rather small. So trying to tell too much in a small area of the box can overwhelm the total design and make it very unappealing. Of course there are always going to be different styles and specific branding that comes from the heart of the person creating the brand. I think you have to keep a few important points in mind, such as the following:

- Keep the font or style clean and easy to read.
- Use distinctive colors, meaning ones that your graphic artist and you have developed as a custom color if possible.
- Choose a high-quality paper for your box or label. This is not an area to get cheaply done in order to save money just because the box is going to be thrown out. Big mistake when you've got a quality product inside.
- Do not put too much information or words on the outside box or on the main component of the product. You need space for ingredients, directions, and a few lines to position how great the product is. Don't overdo it. Make sure your website is on the packaging so that you can give your consumer more information there.

- Quality control is imperative when dealing with packaging. It's common for entrepreneurs or startup people to assume that the packaging or the bottle or the cap are all going to arrive and be perfect. In fact, they seldom are. So be sure to check your shipments when they arrive or be at the press run when your boxes are being printed. Do everything you can to get assurance from your supplier that they will stand behind their product for you.

- Brochures or any other promotional material you want to give to the customer should look as good as your packaging, and it should match it as much as possible. Here again, don't fill the brochure with too much information or too little. You don't have to go overboard on the expense of the paper but make sure it's durable enough to withstand the handling it will endure.

- Photos: spend the money to find a good photographer who knows how to photograph products, not style ads, but products. The photos should have clean lighting that enhances the image of your brand and/ or photos of consumers demonstrating how your product looks when used. Here, too, quality is very important to add to your image.

I once had a client who was extremely creative and developed an amazing nail polish and packaged it in a really cool customized-design bottle. He priced it for a department-store-type customer so he had some margin to allow him to pay for a box to put it in. Even the box that he designed was a creative endeavor and added to his overall image of his brand. But he went to a supplier in China to get the best price for making his boxes. Unfortunately, the shipment that came in was not the proper color black but a strange shade of black with a green tone because quality inks were not used. The paper quality of the box was not good either, and ultimately they became shopworn very easily once they were placed inside stores. So that was money down the drain, as well as time to get them manufactured again properly. I rest my case.

Don't get me wrong, I believe you have to shop around for the best prices for the best quality. But that should be your mission, rather than to just go out seeking the best price only. People get caught up in that vicious cycle of finding the cheapest price.

All of your materials that represent your brand should have consistency of quality and image. So your press kits, business cards, letterhead, and particularly your website all should have the same feeling and images to represent your brand at its best. If you feel that graphic area is not your strong suit then rely on your graphic artist and friends or family that you feel will give you objective criticism.

Now let's take a look at the imagery that is associated with your website.

Chapter Ten

Your Brand's Website

Your single most important marketing element is your website.

Back in 1997, I was working in the Federated Department Stores buying offices as a corporate manager of the fragrance and cosmetics division. The internet world for ecommerce was just getting started. I didn't consider myself a geek, but I knew our lives would change once the internet began to teach us all the possibilities. After long hours at work I went home and thought about this internet business as a potential way to sell beauty products. I thought of all the busy women like myself who often had to replace beauty products that they already knew they liked but had no real time to shop. You would think working in New York City near so many department stores would give me easy access to shopping, but my life was consumed with work that kept me at my desk. And I thought about all the other women who were busy at home with kids, trying to find some time for themselves, which I knew usually happened very late at night after the kids were in bed.

I immediately thought I had to get involved in creating an internet site for the company I worked for: Federated Department Stores. Now we take it for granted that if we can find something in the store then we will most likely find it on a website. We also know now that the website that represents a brand can give us more detailed information about the product we are looking for, how it works, what its ingredients are, and even how other people like or dislike it in their reviews. After realizing that a website might be able to help us sell more products for Federated Department Stores, the company I represented, I immediately set about making my presentation to the CEO, who at the time was Terry Lundgren. Unfortunately security of the credit cards over the internet at this time was not secure. But Terry saw the vision of getting started with this new world and the cosmetics category was probably one of the best to use to reach out to our female customers. So I went about the task of putting together a beauty website that would belong to Federated Department Stores. We trademarked the name Beauty Focus. I managed to get some of the major cosmetic and fragrance brands that sold to Federated to be part of this new internet project of mine. They agreed to participate in this as a new marketing approach. So off I went and created the initial website of the "Beauty Focus." Looking back on the project it seems strange that I was able to pull that off. It did turn out to be a great marketing tool, but ultimately the inability to make sales from it due to the credit card security problem made it difficult to sustain the project.

From the very beginning of the internet world of ecommerce I knew that it would be an important communication tool, as well as profitable towards anything in the beauty business. Today I tell my clients it is extremely important for them to create a website for their brand. Consumers are different today than they were even ten years ago. They want to know more about the products they are buying. It has become extremely important with the beauty business because consumers want to know what ingredients are in a product and if they buy it what will it do for them. You could basically say that consumers today are more demanding than ever before. But I think that it's a good thing that we have to stay on our toes to be sure that the brand we make is exciting as well as safe.

Many people don't realize that your brand's website is a place that buyers will check out first before they even have you present your product line to them. They will make evaluations about how good your product may be or how capable you are going into business with them simply by looking at the website. The days of putting up a simple name, picture, and contact information to qualify as a website in the beauty business is no longer acceptable. You have to consider the website as an extension of your entire image of your brand just as you would the packaging or the logo of your product. It's all connected. There are a number of points that I share with my clients about how to create a great website for their brand. The following are some of those points:

- Make sure the photos that you put on your website are crisp, clear, and have the proper resolution. A photographer who is adept at taking photographs of products will help you with this.
- Use a lot of white background when you are showing photographs of your brand, such as on the individual page selling the product. I have noticed many people want to overdesign their website sometimes, just as they do packaging; be careful not to do that. Photographs should be really beautiful rather than placed against an overdesigned background. Again, keep everything consistent. Your logo should be sized on the website appropriately and should look exactly as you have designed it in your packaging.
- There is another element of design and websites to be cautious of. Many website designers happen to be men. And many men tend to make their websites look very gray or mechanical. Instruct your web designer to not go in this direction unless it truly connects with the way you designed your product. There are many good sites today that help you to design your own site and I have used them occasionally to great

success but you have to feel sure that you know how to be creative. If you are up for it . . . it's inexpensive and worth a try.

- Be sure your website is easy to shop. Too many people who are web designers get caught in all the fun aspects of fancy Flash design or things that they think look interesting but in fact keep the consumer from making their decision and closing their sale. Be sure that website visitors can find ingredients easily, prices, and how to check out as easily as they can.

- Put your website address on your business cards, your stationary, and your packaging. Take every opportunity you can to let people know where to find your product.

- It would be OK to be moderately promotional on your own website. It's not going to deter a retailer from doing business with you as long as you're not deeply discounting your product on a frequent basis. The money that you make off of your website is always going to be a higher profit margin than what you get when you have to sell to retail. So increasing your own website business is particularly important financially. Building up your database or, rather, all that will sign up to get emails from you directly from your site is important to do, but you may have to be patient while that happens organically one year at a time.

- If your website is essentially the only place that someone can find and purchase your product then obviously you have to reach out and really promote your website in every way possible. If your business plan calls for you to be distributed in retail locations, particularly larger ones, then you may find that your own website is not going to do a lot of business for you. Many of my clients are surprised at this. They assume that their own website will be very active. The fact is many consumers would rather purchase products from a known source, such as a department store website or Amazon.com, rather than the brand's own website. Sometimes it's a matter of trust, and other times it's a matter of fact that they can shop for more things on a larger website such as Amazon. I actually do recommend that most people try to put their products up on Amazon.com. At the very least, it's a place that people may find your product quickly considering how many people shop for products on Amazon.com and often are able to get reduced or free shipping because of their loyalty. I know of one men's grooming line that became so large on Amazon that it was asked to go into retail stores.

There are so many other points about website business in the beauty category that I could find myself writing a separate book about it. There are some brands in beauty that just do it really well, and I often recommend that everyone should go on the internet and simply go to all the websites of products that they admire and see how they designed that website. It would be best to choose some brands that are not necessarily so big that they are globally known. Of course, take a look at them, but realize that they have built their name up to be so large that they can take a lot of creative license. They can make their website be more of a positioning statement rather than a shopping website. Of course you should make your website your own, but don't be afraid to take some direction from websites that you know are really good.

Now Go Forth and
Be Successful!

Well now all you have to do is put all these pieces together, dig deep within yourself and make your business tremendously successful! Remember that this is a process and a journey. Keep your vision on how you see the outcome of all your hard work. You may have a few learning curves to experience but that's okay because it's part of the process. The beauty business is exciting and lucrative. Seize the moment, and go for it!

If you want to reach out and ask me a question, you can do that by posting it on the message board of my website devoted specifically to this book: Www.beautyentrepreneurs. com This website will also have an area where beauty entrepreneurs can chat with each other and feel a sense of camaraderie. I plan to include a place on the website where I can recommend resources and suppliers that I feel are good to do business with.

I truly wish great success to everyone reading this book. I wrote this book in order to share my experiences with all beauty entrepreneurs. There has never been a greater time then now to step out and create your ideas and be your own boss. If you're up for the challenge, you are in for an amazing ride.

About Michelle F. Williams

Michelle Williams is a native New Yorker who began her retail career at Abraham and Straus, a regional New York department store, where she held the positions of both cosmetics and fragrance buyer for a number of years in the mid 1980s. She went on to become a fragrance and cosmetics buyer for the national chain Lord & Taylor, and eventually was recruited to become the Divisional Merchandise Manager of fragrances for Bloomingdale's stores where she remained for three years.

In 1992 Ms. Williams became the Corporate VP of cosmetics for Federated Department Stores, responsible for the corporate management of the cosmetics business with a volume of $1.8 billion dollars. While in this position she reported directly to the Chairman of Federated Merchandising.

In 1996, she recognized the importance of the internet and its potential. She created and launched the first prestige beauty website on the internet in 1996, named *Beauty Focus*, which also had a magazine aspect to it. In 1997 she took over the VP of Cosmetics position for Macy's West in San Francisco, which at that time was the single-largest cosmetics division in Federated Department Stores Corporation and the United States.

By 1999 she decided to leave the department store world and took her years of experience as a merchant to begin her own cosmetics consulting company, Michelle Williams Group LLC, located in New York City. Ms. Williams was part of the founding and development team of a new website, Beauty.com. She made the deal for an exclusive contract with the famous makeup artist Kevyn Aucoin, to write a column for the site. She designed the consumer-friendly architecture in the site and helped to complete the site in less than six months. Shortly after the site sold to Drugstore.com

A few years later, she became the President and COO of Kevyn Aucoin Cosmetics company where she developed business plans and helped to raise funds for the start-up of the company, she also was involved in the selection of the suppliers for the brand and developing its ecommerce web site.

In 2004 Ms. Williams returned to consulting various aspects of the beauty industry with a focus on emerging brands both domestic and international. Her passion continues in her work with the love of new businesses and ideas and, of course, working with entrepreneurs.

www.michellewilliamsgroup.com